D1442251

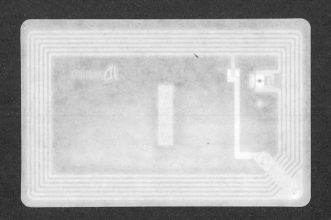

TWO MEN AND A CAR

Franklin Roosevelt, Al Capone, and a Cadillac V-8

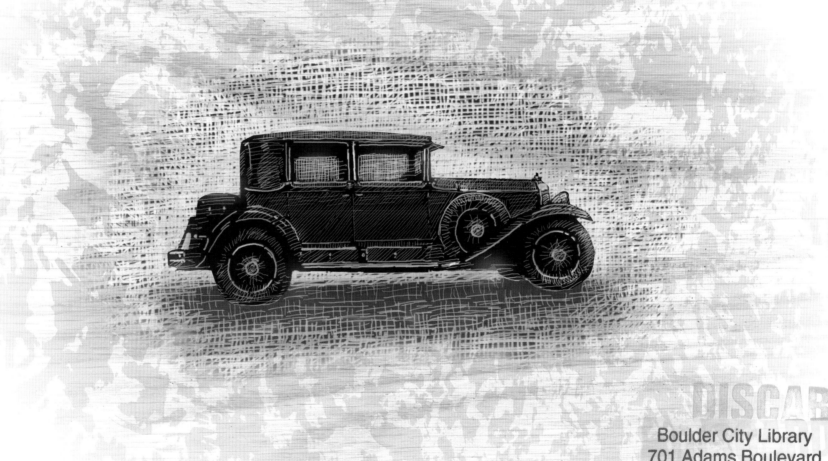

MICHAEL GARLAND

This tale begins as a story about a car.

Then it becomes a story about the lives of two men.

And finally it becomes a story about America
in the first half of the twentieth century.

But it begins with a car.

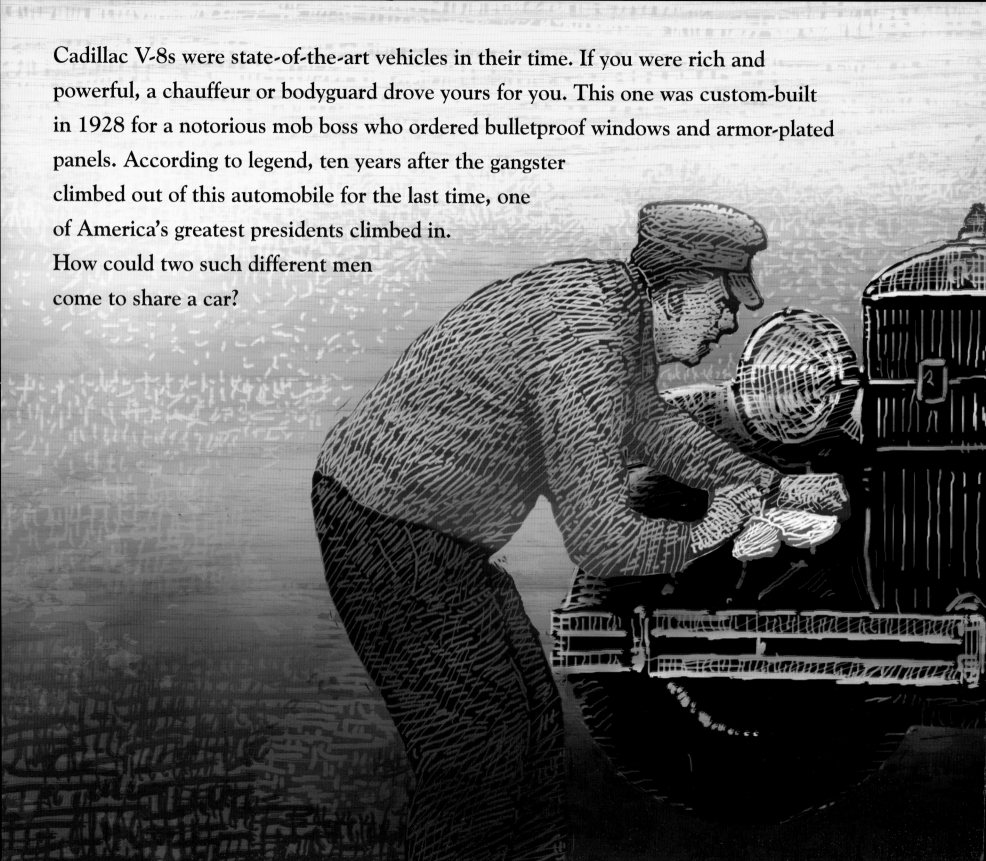

Cadillac V-8s were state-of-the-art vehicles in their time. If you were rich and powerful, a chauffeur or bodyguard drove yours for you. This one was custom-built in 1928 for a notorious mob boss who ordered bulletproof windows and armor-plated panels. According to legend, ten years after the gangster climbed out of this automobile for the last time, one of America's greatest presidents climbed in. How could two such different men come to share a car?

The future president, Franklin Delano Roosevelt, was born in Hyde Park, New York in 1882. His Dutch ancestors had immigrated to New York before 1650 and bought forty-eight acres of prime real estate in what is now midtown Manhattan. Their descendants became wealthy and prominent over the following two centuries.

Franklin was the only child of James and Sara Roosevelt. When he was a toddler, his doting mother kept his hair long and dressed him in frilly gowns, a common practice back then.

Franklin traveled with his family to Europe, where he learned to speak French and German. He played golf and polo. When he was sixteen, his father gave him a sailboat named *New Moon* that Franklin piloted through the tide-swept waters surrounding the Roosevelts' summer estate on Campobello Island, Canada, just offshore from eastern Maine.

Alphonse Capone, the future mob boss, was born in Brooklyn, New York in 1899, five years after his parents immigrated to New York from Italy and just a few days before Franklin Roosevelt's seventeenth birthday.

This is Al.

Alphonse's father, Gabriele, was a barber, and his mother, Teresa, worked as a seamstress. Alphonse was one of nine children. His family and friends called him Al.

Al was a quick learner, but he hated his school's unbending discipline and harsh punishments. At age fourteen he was expelled for hitting a teacher, and from that point on, he got his education on the streets of New York City. He worked in a candy store and a bowling alley, then joined a youth gang. Then he graduated to the Five Points Gang of criminals in Lower Manhattan.

Five Points gang members.

Franklin attended Groton, an exclusive boarding school in Massachusetts. Then, like many of his Groton classmates, he went to Harvard University. He wasn't a top student, but he was chosen to edit the *Harvard Crimson* daily newspaper because of his leadership ability. He graduated from college in 1903, when Al Capone was four years old.

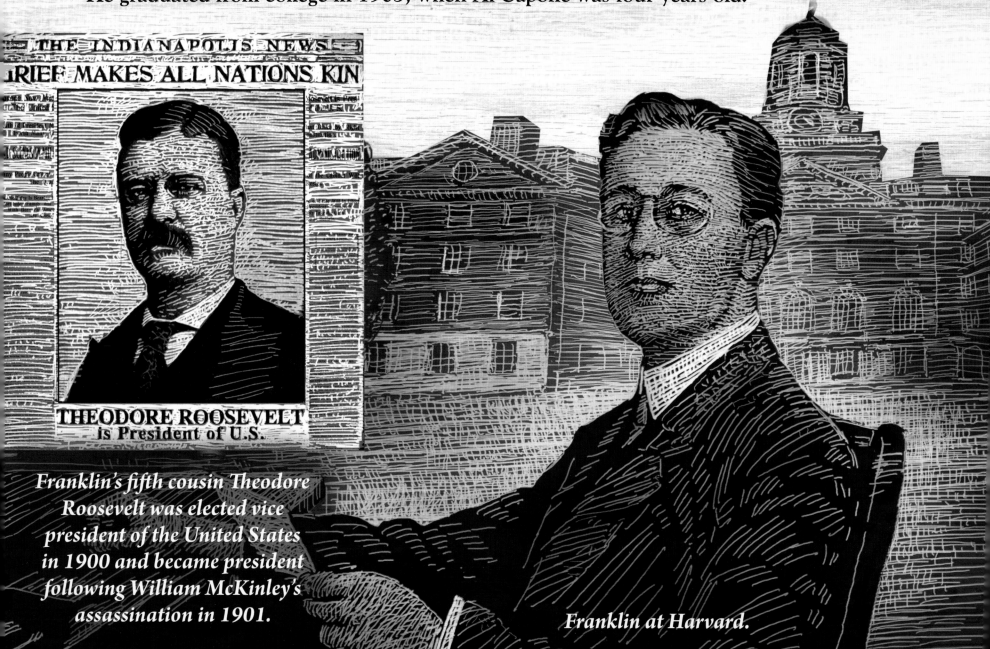

THE INDIANAPOLIS NEWS

RIEF MAKES ALL NATIONS KIN

THEODORE ROOSEVELT
is President of U.S.

Franklin's fifth cousin Theodore Roosevelt was elected vice president of the United States in 1900 and became president following William McKinley's assassination in 1901.

Franklin at Harvard.

The Harvard Inn was a dancehall and saloon in the seaside Brooklyn neighborhood of Coney Island. Al worked there at age eighteen as a bouncer and bartender for racketeer Frankie Yale. Al received a knife wound to his cheek during a fight there, and the nickname Scarface would stay with him the rest of his life.

Al in Coney Island.

In 1905, when he was twenty-three, Franklin married distant cousin Eleanor Roosevelt. President Theodore Roosevelt gave his favorite niece's hand in marriage. Franklin studied law, worked for a Wall Street firm, and in 1910 was elected a New York State senator. President Woodrow Wilson appointed him assistant secretary of the U.S. Navy in 1913, and he served in that position through World War I. That's what Franklin was doing when Al got the cut that made him Scarface.

Theodore.

Franklin inspecting a ship.

In 1918, at age nineteen, Al married Mae Josephine Coughlin, and together they had a baby, Albert Francis, whom they nicknamed Sonny. Crime boss Johnny Torrio was the boy's godfather. The Capones moved to Baltimore, where Al found work as a bookkeeper for a construction company. This was a chance for him to become a law-abiding American like most of his boyhood friends in Brooklyn, but Al didn't choose that life.

Roosevelt in front of the townhouse on East 65th Street, Manhattan, where he and Eleanor lived beginning in 1908.

Franklin Roosevelt, the future president, and Al Capone, the future mob boss, had things in common. Both were smart and ambitious. Both were young when their fathers died: Franklin was eighteen and Al was twenty-one. They may have passed each other in the streets of New York. But they were headed in opposite directions.

Capone on the streets of the Bowery in Lower Manhattan.

A big influence on Franklin's choices was his headmaster at Groton School, who taught the importance of public service. Franklin campaigned against Tammany Hall, the corrupt organization that controlled politics in New York State.

Franklin with Endicott Peabody, headmaster of Groton.

A big influence on Al was Johnny Torrio, who was the boss of the Five Points Gang before moving to Chicago. The gang helped Tammany Hall hold onto power by stuffing ballot boxes and intimidating voters, and Tammany Hall looked the other way while gang members ran their criminal rackets.

Al with Johnny Torrio.

In 1919, the Eighteenth Amendment to the U.S. Constitution outlawed the sale and consumption of alcohol. This began the Prohibition Era and created big opportunities for criminals. In 1920 Al Capone joined Johnny Torrio in Chicago to help run Torrio's crime syndicate there.

Prohibition agents dumping barrels of beer.

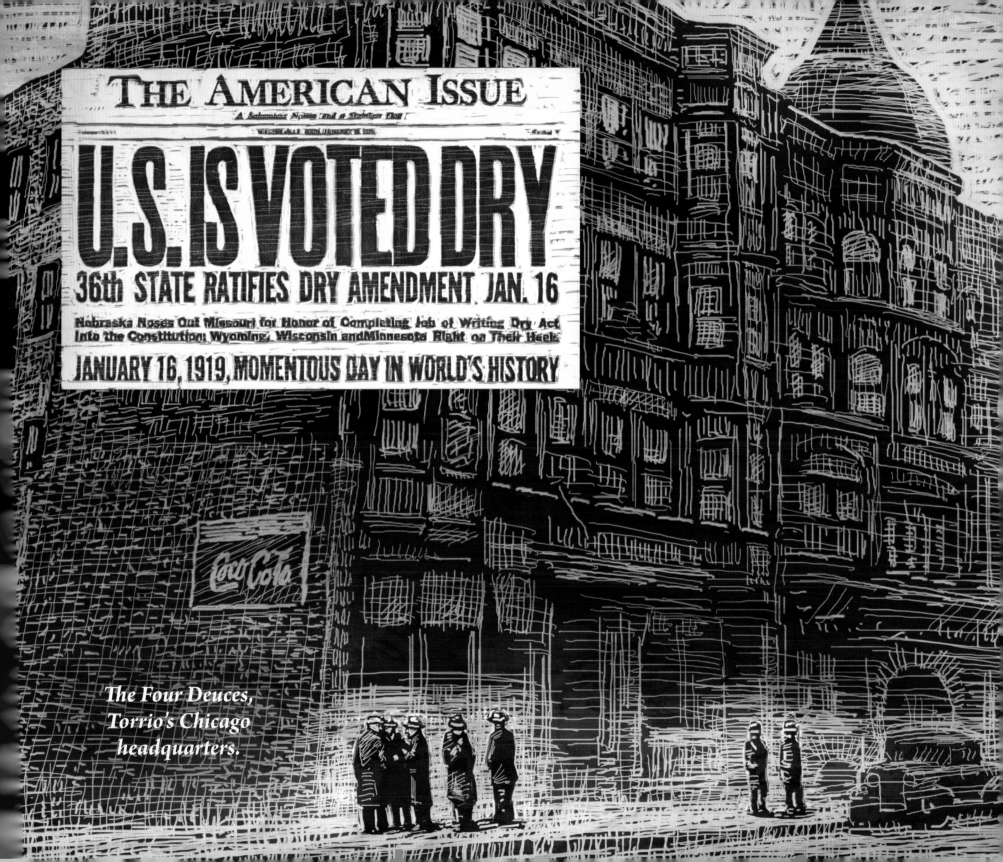

THE AMERICAN ISSUE

U.S. IS VOTED DRY

36th STATE RATIFIES DRY AMENDMENT JAN. 16

Nebraska Noses Out Missouri for Honor of Completing Job of Writing Dry Act Into the Constitution; Wyoming, Wisconsin and Minnesota Right on Their Heels

JANUARY 16, 1919, MOMENTOUS DAY IN WORLD'S HISTORY

The Four Deuces, Torrio's Chicago headquarters.

Roosevelt (right) campaigning with James Cox.

Franklin Roosevelt's family connections and charisma boosted him through the ranks of the Democratic Party. He was nominated for vice president of the United States on the 1920 Democratic ticket, but he and presidential nominee James Cox lost in a landslide. The next year Roosevelt was stricken with what doctors diagnosed as polio, and it left him partially paralyzed for the rest of his life. By then, Franklin and Eleanor and their children were living at Springwood, the beautiful Roosevelt estate in Hyde Park.

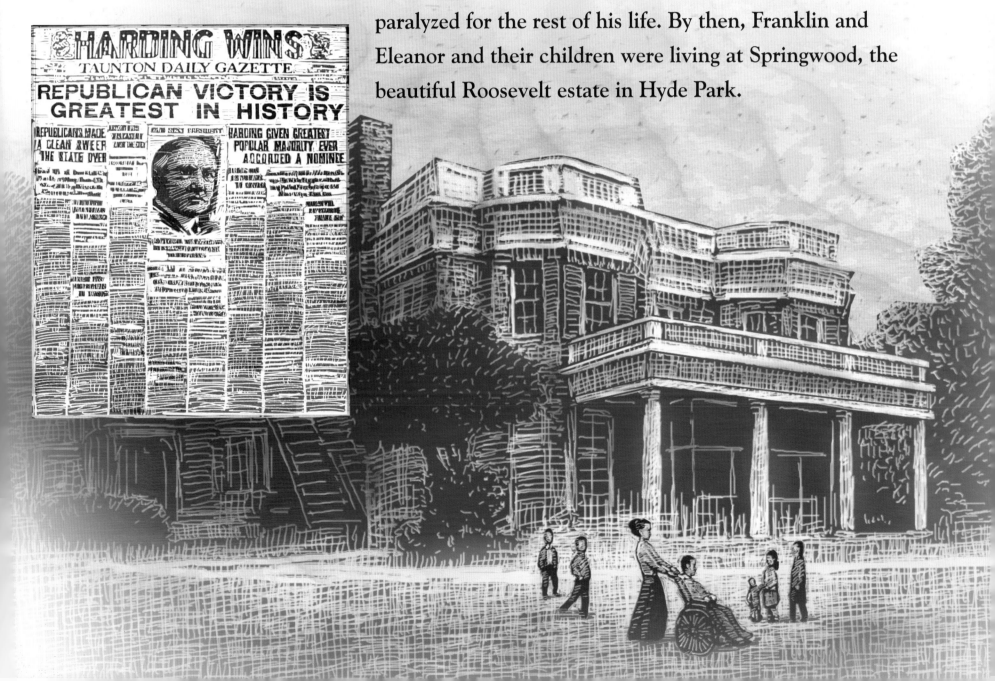

HARDING WINS

TAUNTON DAILY GAZETTE

REPUBLICAN VICTORY IS GREATEST IN HISTORY

REPUBLICANS MADE A CLEAN SWEEP THE STATE OVER

HARDING GIVEN GREATEST POPULAR MAJORITY EVER ACCORDED A NOMINEE

With Johnny Torrio's help, Capone rose quickly through the Chicago underworld. By the time his wife, son, mother, younger brothers, and sister joined him in Chicago in 1923, he was set on a life of crime. Joined by two of his brothers, Al became a boss in the dog-eat-dog rackets of gambling, vice, and bootlegged whiskey. He made many enemies.

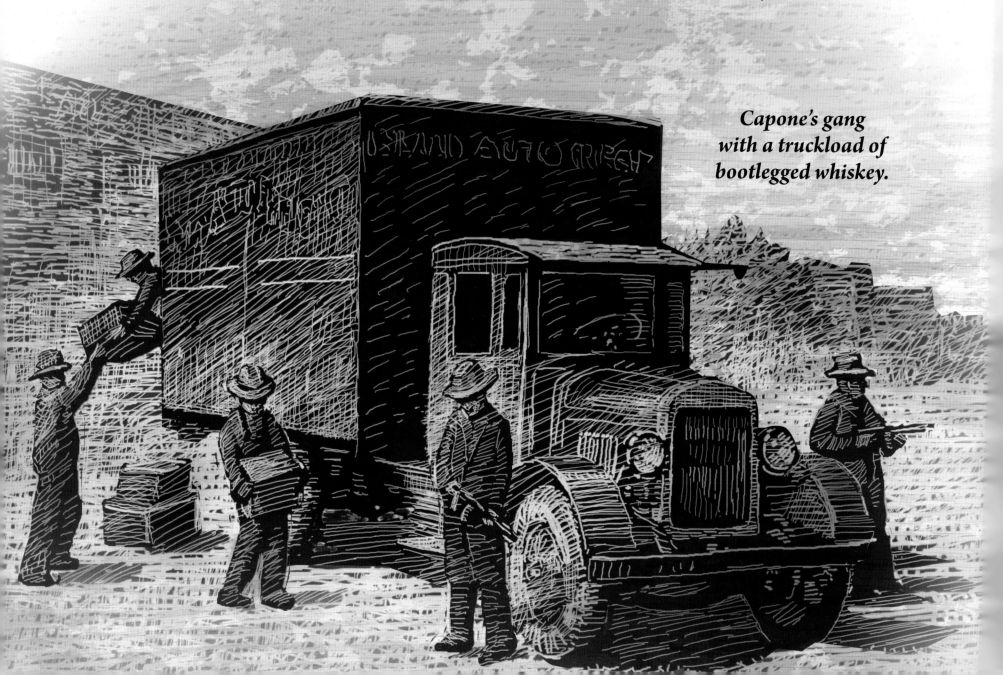

Capone's gang with a truckload of bootlegged whiskey.

Roosevelt was a determined politician who fought his opponents with ballots. He learned to walk again with the help of leg braces and canes, and he managed to hide the severity of his disability from the public. In 1928 he was narrowly elected governor of New York.

★ FOR GOVERNOR ★

FRANKLIN D. ROOSEVELT

KEEP GOOD GOVERNMENT

Capone was a determined gangster who fought his opponents with guns. He committed or ordered multiple murders by the mid-1920s. His criminal activities raked in big money. He wore expensive suits and jewelry, and he could easily afford the bulletproof Cadillac that he bought in 1928 for his protection.

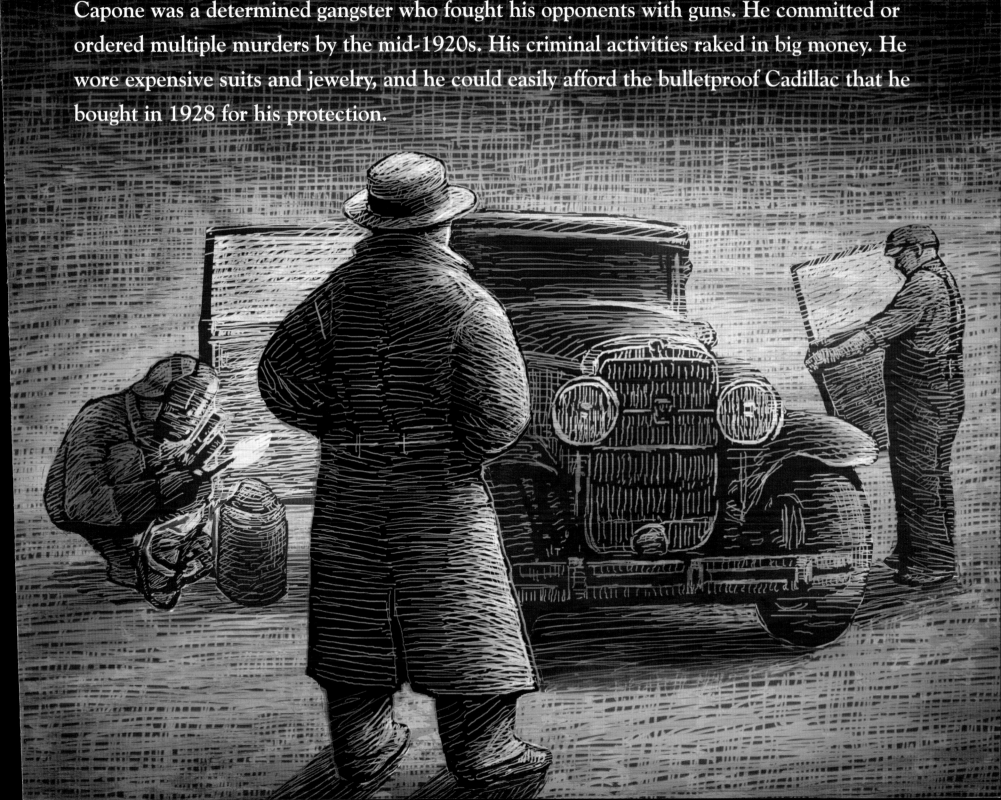

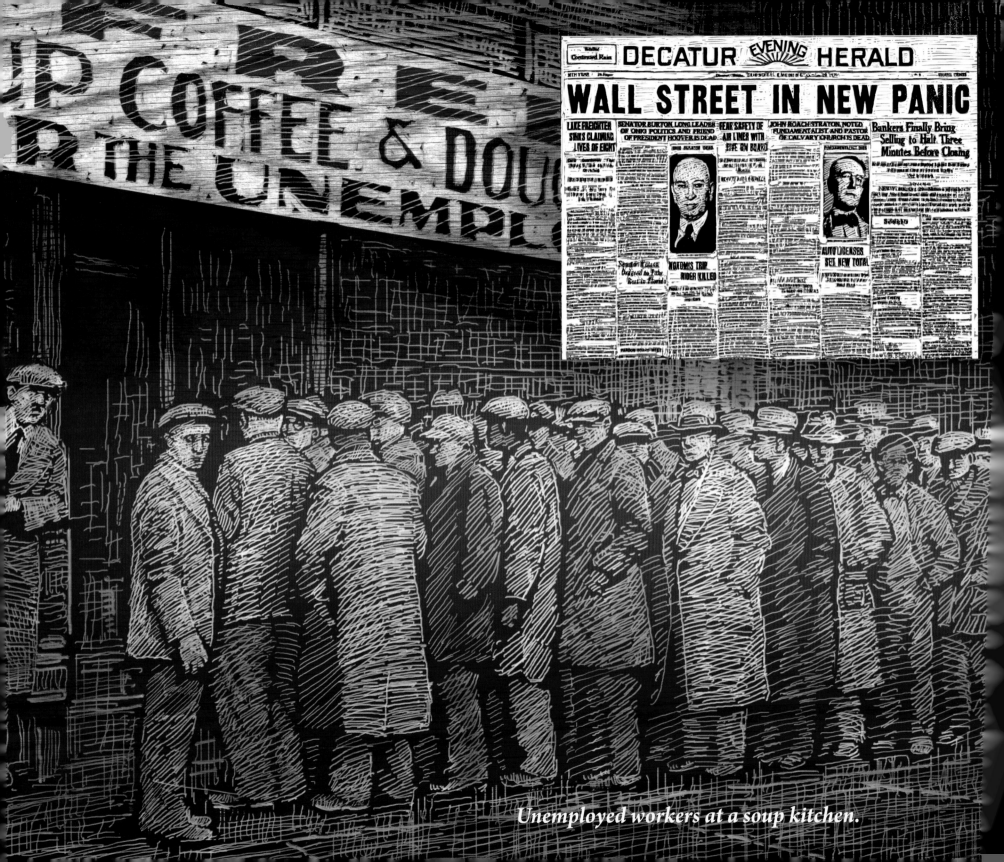

DECATUR EVENING HERALD

WALL STREET IN NEW PANIC

Unemployed workers at a soup kitchen.

Roosevelt used influence and persuasion to maintain his grip on New York politics. After the Wall Street Crash of 1929, he urged the U.S. government to offer unemployment insurance. He spoke directly with voters in radio broadcasts that he called "fireside chats." In his second run for governor in 1930, he called for old-age pensions and aid to farmers. This time he won by a wide margin.

Capone used bribery and violence to maintain a grip on his criminal empire in Chicago. In 1929 he committed his most notorious crime, the Saint Valentine's Day Massacre. He sent gang members dressed as police to a garage where a rival, Bugs Moran, was expected to be. Moran escaped, but seven members of his gang were lined up against a wall and killed.

Capone was at his Florida estate when the massacre happened, but no one was fooled. He acquired a new nickname, Public Enemy Number One. He needed his bulletproof car more than ever.

Eliot Ness.

In 1929, an eleven-member task force was hand-picked by federal agent Eliot Ness to bring Capone to justice. They were called The Untouchables because Capone wasn't able to bribe them as he had bribed Chicago police, judges, and politicians. In 1931 Capone was convicted of tax evasion and sentenced to eleven years in prison plus fines, court costs, and back taxes totaling $272,690 (equivalent to about $3.5 million today). The government confiscated his bulletproof Cadillac.

Franklin Roosevelt was the Democratic presidential candidate in 1932 and defeated Herbert Hoover, the incumbent Republican. The Great Depression was making people hungry and afraid all over the world. President-elect Roosevelt narrowly escaped assassination by an anarchist in Florida. The mayor of Chicago was mortally wounded while sitting next to Franklin.

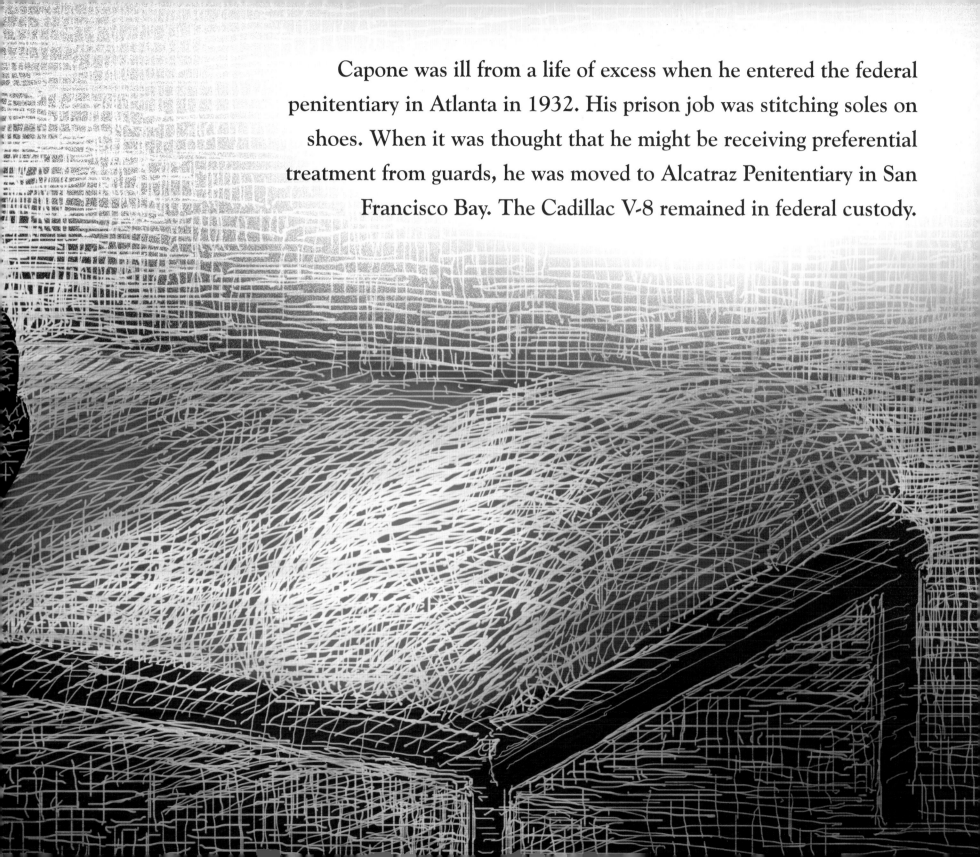

Capone was ill from a life of excess when he entered the federal penitentiary in Atlanta in 1932. His prison job was stitching soles on shoes. When it was thought that he might be receiving preferential treatment from guards, he was moved to Alcatraz Penitentiary in San Francisco Bay. The Cadillac V-8 remained in federal custody.

In his March 1933 Inaugural Address, President Franklin Roosevelt told Americans that "the only thing we have to fear is fear itself." He enacted a series of programs to generate economic growth and relief from poverty, calling this the New Deal. He made Wall Street reforms. The country seemed to be emerging from the Depression in the late 1930s when a new threat loomed: the rising power and aggression of Japan and Nazi Germany.

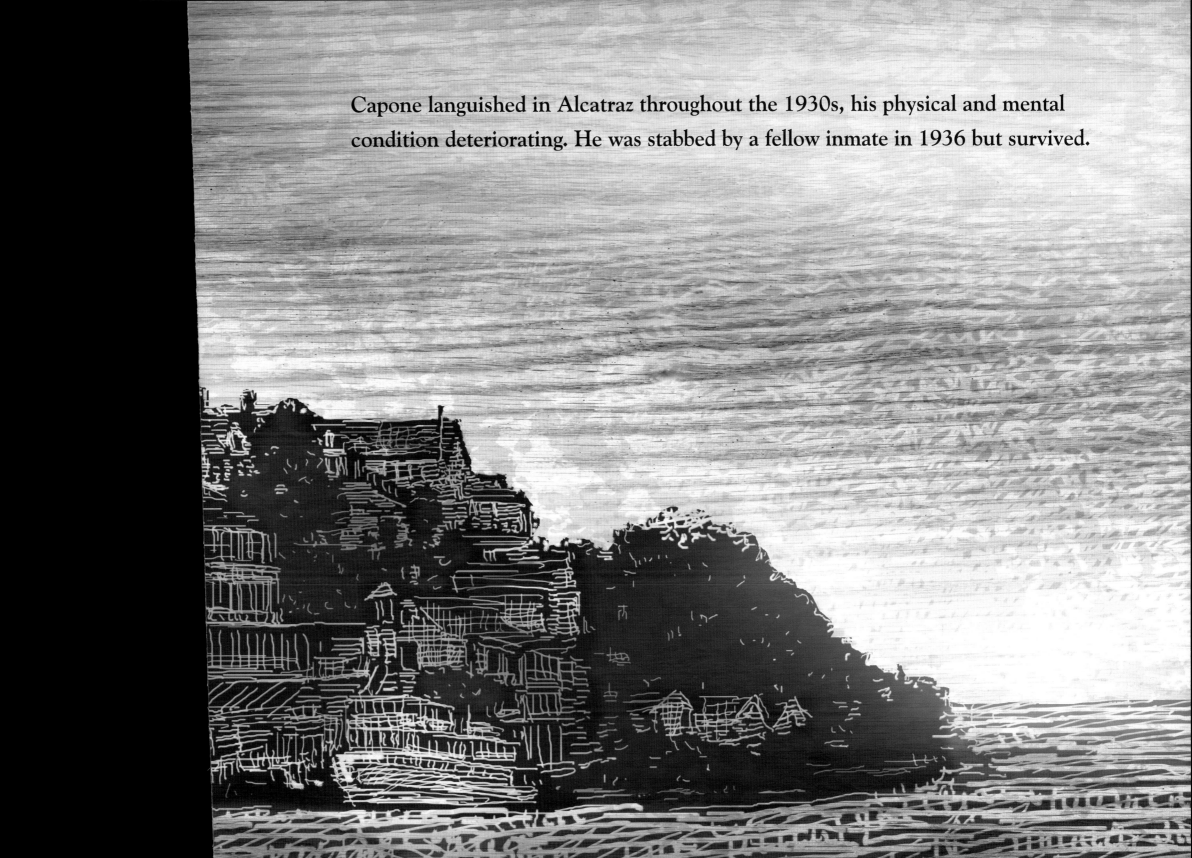

Capone languished in Alcatraz throughout the 1930s, his physical and mental condition deteriorating. He was stabbed by a fellow inmate in 1936 but survived.

On December 7, 1941, the Japanese launched a surprise attack on the U.S. naval base in Pearl Harbor, Hawaii. This is when the legend of the 1928 Cadillac began.

The next day Michael F. Reilly, one of Roosevelt's Secret Service men, was tasked with transporting the president down Pennsylvania Avenue from the White House to the Capitol Building, where Roosevelt would make his historic "Day of Infamy" speech and ask Congress to declare war on Japan.

Reilly later wrote that the government had no armored car in which to transport the president. According to Reilly, someone suggested taking Al Capone's Cadillac out of the impound lot and pressing it into service.

Franklin Roosevelt died in April 1945, eleven weeks into his fourth term as president, after leading the country through the Depression and World War II.

The *New York Times* declared, "Men will thank God on their knees a hundred years from now that Franklin D. Roosevelt was in the White House." Three hundred thousand people lined the streets of Washington, D.C. to watch his flag-draped coffin pass by. He was buried in the rose garden of his Hyde Park estate.

Al Capone was released from prison in 1939, feeble with illness. He spent his last years at his Florida estate with severe dementia, dying at age forty-eight in 1947, less than two years after Roosevelt.

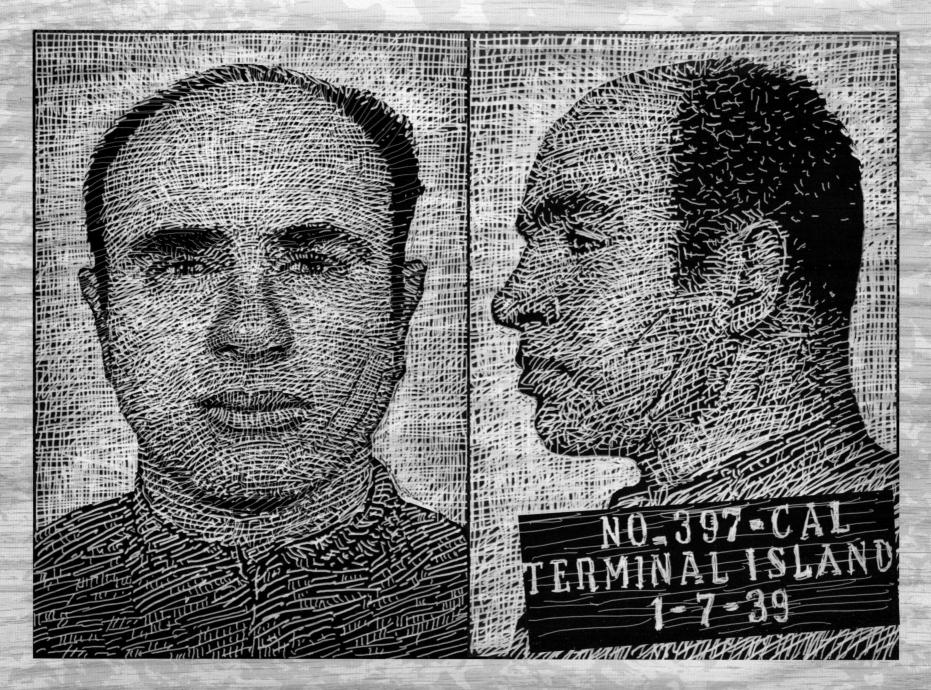

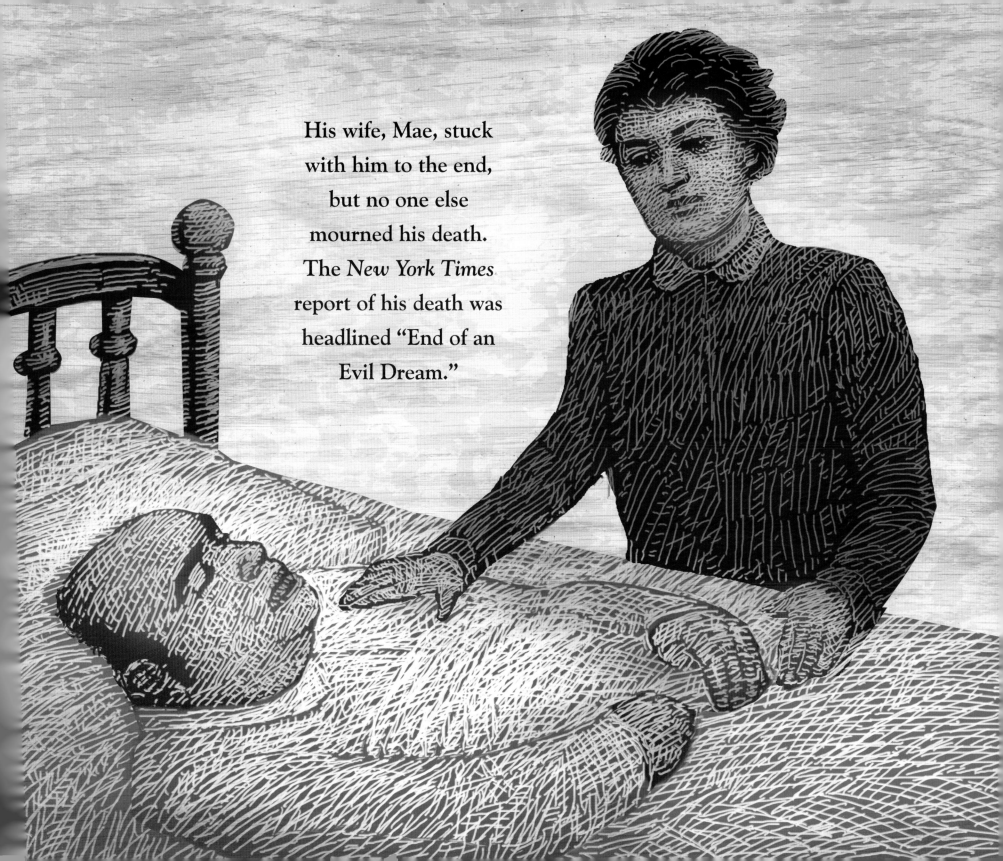

His wife, Mae, stuck with him to the end, but no one else mourned his death. The *New York Times* report of his death was headlined "End of an Evil Dream."

Did Franklin Roosevelt really ride in Al Capone's car the day he delivered one of the most important speeches in U.S. history? This urban legend persists despite the absence of much confirming evidence. Whatever the truth of the matter, it provides a way to contrast the lives of two Americans in the first half of the twentieth century, one a great leader and one a notorious mobster.

Author's Note

The story of FDR's ride to the U.S. Capitol in Al Capone's bulletproof gangster car is the subject of much debate. There are inconsistencies in Secret Serviceman Michael F. Reilly's description and account of the event, and there are conflicting stories about what became of the car after its release from federal custody. I've chosen to leave those controversies unresolved and focus instead on the lives of President Franklin Delano Roosevelt and Scarface Al Capone, two Americans who shared headlines in the first half of the twentieth century.

—Michael Garland

A ROOSEVELT-CAPONE TIMELINE

1882: Franklin Roosevelt, an only child, is born on January 30 in Hyde Park, New York, to wealthy parents James Roosevelt and Sara Ann Delano.

1884: Still a toddler, Franklin travels to Europe with his parents, the first of many such trips.

1891: Franklin attends public school in Germany.

1894: Gabriele and Teresa Capone are among the thousands of Italian emigrants who pass through the immigration inspection station on Ellis Island in New York Harbor.

1896: Franklin attends the Groton School in Groton, Massachusetts.

1898: Franklin adds sailing to his recreational pursuits of riding, shooting, and playing tennis and golf.

1899: Alphonse Capone, one of Gabriele and Teresa's nine children, is born on January 17 in Brooklyn, New York.

1900: Roosevelt attends Harvard College in Cambridge, Massachusetts. His father dies.

1901: Roosevelt's fifth cousin Theodore Roosevelt serves six months as the vice president of the United States, then becomes the nation's twenty-sixth president when President William McKinley is assassinated in September.

1905: Roosevelt marries fifth cousin, once removed, Eleanor Roosevelt on March 17, moves to New York, and enrolls in Columbia Law School. The couple will have six children, one of whom, Franklin, dies in infancy in 1909. (A second Franklin is born in 1914.)

1907: Roosevelt drops out of law school after passing the New York bar exam.

1908: Roosevelt joins a Wall Street law firm and begins practicing admiralty law, but he tells friends he wants a career in politics.

1910: Roosevelt is elected to the New York State Senate on November 8. He is a Democrat like his deceased father, even

though his hero Theodore Roosevelt is a Republican. He imme-diately begins opposing the Tammany Hall political machine that controls the New York State Democratic Party.

1912: Roosevelt wins reelection to the New York State Senate despite being bedridden with typhoid fever for a month during the campaign.

1913: Roosevelt is appointed assistant secretary of the U.S. Navy by President Woodrow Wilson and resigns his New York State Senate seat to travel to Washington, DC. He will serve as assis-tant secretary for the duration of World War I.

1913: Al is expelled from school for hitting a teacher.

1913 to 1917: Al joins street gangs in Brooklyn and is eventu-ally accepted to membership in the Five Points Gang in Lower Manhattan.

1914: Roosevelt loses a campaign to be the Democratic Party nominee for U.S. Senator from New York.

1914: World War I breaks out in Europe in July, but the U.S. remains neutral.

1917: Congress declares war on Germany on April 6 after Ger-man submarines sink several U.S. merchant ships. Roosevelt wants to serve as an active-duty naval officer, but President Woodrow Wilson insists that he continue as assistant secretary.

1917: Capone receives a slash wound to the face while working for gangster Frankie Yale as a bouncer at the Harvard Ballroom in Coney Island. The incident leaves him with his lifelong nick-name, Scarface.

1918: Capone marries Mae Josephine Coughlin. They have one child.

1918: The armistice of November 11 ends World War I with Germany's defeat.

1919: The Eighteenth Amendment to the U.S. Constitution, outlawing the production, transport, and sale of alcoholic beverages, is fully ratified on January 16.

1920: Nationwide enforcement of the Volstead Act, enacting the Eighteenth Amendment, begins on January 17, initiating the thirteen-year Prohibition era.

1920: The Nineteenth Amendment to the U.S. Constitution, ratified on August 18, grants women the right to vote.

1920: Capone moves to Chicago following the death of his father to work for gangster Johnny Torrio. With the dawn of Prohibition, Torrio's gang begins bootlegging—illegally distilling, transporting, and selling alcohol.

1920: Governor James Cox of Ohio wins the Democratic Party's presidential nomination and selects Roosevelt as his running mate, but their ticket is beaten badly in the general election.

1921: Roosevelt is stricken with a severe illness during a vacation on Campobello Island, New Brunswick. Though diagnosed as polio at the time, the illness might have been Guillain-Barré syndrome. He is left permanently paralyzed from the waist down.

1923: Torrio and Capone move their headquarters to Cicero, Illinois, a Chicago suburb, where they can bribe local politicians and buy protection.

1925: Capone takes over Johnny Torrio's mob when Torrio retires following an assassination attempt. Speakeasies (illegal saloons)

have proliferated, and bootlegging is big business for the mob. Capone's criminal activities net a reported $60 million per year over the next few years, the equivalent of $840 million per year in 2018 dollars.

1926: Roosevelt establishes a polio treatment facility in Warm Springs, Georgia, and continues undergoing treatments. Determined to resume his political career and convinced he'll be unelectable if confined to a wheelchair, he conditions himself to walk short distances while wearing steel leg braces and using a cane.

1926: Capone is eating lunch at his Hawthorne Hotel headquarters in Cicero on September 20 when the North Side Gang led by Hymie Weiss and Bugs Moran attempts to assassinate him. The attempt is unsuccessful, and Weiss is machine-gunned to death the following month by suspected Capone gang members.

1928: Roosevelt is narrowly elected governor of New York on November 6, winning by less than one percent of the vote.

1928: Capone buys a mansion in Palm Island, Florida.

1929: On February 14, four Capone gang members (two of them disguised as police) enter a garage and order seven men, including six members of Bugs Moran's gang, to line up against a wall, where they are shot to death. Moran narrowly escapes what becomes known as the Saint Valentine's Day Massacre.

1929: Capone is arrested by FBI agents in March for feigning illness and delaying testimony before a federal grand jury. He posts a $5,000 bond and is released.

1929: U.S. Treasury Department agent Eliot Ness is tasked with bringing Capone to justice. He assembles a team of agents nicknamed "The Untouchables." The team raids illegal stills and breweries and causes major damage to Capone's operations in the following months, but in the end it is the Internal Revenue Service that will bring down Capone.

1929: On May 17, Capone and a bodyguard are arrested and convicted in Philadelphia for carrying concealed weapons.

1929: The stock market crashes on October 29, helping to trigger the Great Depression. President Herbert Hoover, a Republican, believes the economy will recover without government intervention, but Governor Roosevelt believes in activist government and establishes a state employment commission in New York.

1930: Capone is released from prison on March 17.

1930: Running for a second term as governor of New York, Roosevelt calls for aid to farmers, unemployment insurance, and pensions for the elderly. This time his margin of victory is 14 percent.

1931: Convicted of federal tax evasion and Prohibition violations, Capone is sentenced on October 18 to eleven years in federal prison.

1932: Tens of thousands of World War I veterans and their families from across the nation gather in Washington, DC to demand payment of the bonuses promised for their military service by a 1924 act of Congress. Dubbed the Bonus Army, many of these veterans are suffering post-traumatic stress disorder (PTSD, then called "shell shock") from trench warfare, which has made them especially

vulnerable to unemployment in the Great Depression. They pitch camp in a "Hooverville" in Washington (one of many such shantytowns springing up around the country then) while picketing Congress. On July 28, President Hoover orders the U.S. Army to clear out the encampment, and more than a hundred veterans are injured. The episode is a public-relations disaster for Hoover.

1932: Roosevelt wins the Democratic Party nomination for president of the United States in July, promising a "new deal" for the American people. On November 8 he defeats Hoover in a landslide to become the thirty-second president of the United States.

1933: In February, the month before his inauguration, Roosevelt is giving a speech in Miami when a would-be assassin fires five bullets at him. None of the bullets hits Roosevelt, but the mayor of Chicago, who is standing next to him, is killed. This leads to a story that the mayor, Anton Cermak, was the real target, and that the shooter, an Italian immigrant, was hired by Frank Nitti, Capone's successor as head of the Chicago mob. According to this story, Cermak had ordered an assassination attempt on Nitti in late 1932 and was killed in an act of retribution. The story is another point of intersection in the lives of Roosevelt and Capone.

1933: Upon his inauguration on March 4, Roosevelt faces the worst depression in U.S. history. A run on the banks causes bank closures across the country. The unemployment rate has reached 25 percent, and two million Americans are homeless. Roosevelt rushes his New Deal legislation to Congress and establishes new federal agencies to provide relief to Americans and put them back to work.

1933: On December 5, Roosevelt signs the Twenty-First Amendment to the U.S. Constitution, which repeals the Eighteenth Amendment and ends Prohibition.

1934: The first wave of Dust Bowl storms sweeps through the Great Plains. Caused by drought and poor farming practices, the Dust Bowl adds another layer of misery to the Great Depression.

1934: Capone is transferred to Alcatraz, a federal prison on an island in San Francisco Bay.

1935: In Roosevelt's Second New Deal legislation, the federal government establishes the Works Progress Administration (WPA), Social Security, the National Labor Relations Board, and other initiatives. Roosevelt admits that many of his administration's actions to combat the depression are experiments. "It is common sense to take a method and try it," he writes. "If it fails, admit it frankly and try another. But above all, try something."

1936: Roosevelt defeats Republican Alf Landon on November 5 to win election to a second term as president, carrying every state except Maine and Vermont in a landslide election.

1939: World War II begins when Germany invades Poland on September 1. The U.S. remains neutral for now, with a spirit of isolationism dominating domestic politics.

1939: Capone is paroled from federal custody at Terminal Island, California, on November 16 and returns to his Palm Island, Florida mansion.

1940: Germany invades France, crushing French resistance in June.

1940: Alarmed by the Nazi blitzkrieg through Europe, Franklin decides to break a tradition extending all the way back to George Washington and run for a third term as president. Wendell Willkie, his Republican opponent, argues that Roosevelt will drag America into the war, but Roosevelt promises not to do so and wins election to a third term on November 5.

1941: On March 11, Congress approves Roosevelt's Lend-Lease Act to send military and economic aid to Britain and the other Allied nations without entering the war. When Germany invades the Soviet Union in June, the Lend-Lease program is extended to the Soviets as well.

1941: Japan attacks the Pacific Fleet of the U.S. Navy at Pearl Harbor, Hawaii, on December 7. The next day, Roosevelt delivers his Day of Infamy speech to a joint session of Congress, and Congress declares war on Japan. Japan's Axis allies Germany and Italy declare war on the United States on December 11, and Roosevelt signs a declaration of war on those two countries that same day.

1942: On February 19, Roosevelt signs an executive order placing many Japanese Americans in detention camps, an injustice that still looms large in the nation's memory.

1944: Allied troops invade northern France on June 6, which history will remember as D-Day.

1944: Roosevelt defeats Republican Thomas Dewey on November 7 to be elected to a fourth term as U.S. president.

1945: Roosevelt meets Allied leaders Josef Stalin (Soviet Union) and Winston Church (Great Britain) on February 11 at Yalta, a Soviet resort city on the Black Sea, to discuss postwar Europe.

1945: Franklin Delano Roosevelt dies of a cerebral hemorrhage at Warms Springs, Georgia, on April 12.

1945: Nazi Germany surrenders to Allied forces in Europe on May 8.

1945: On August 6 and 9, under orders from President Harry S. Truman, the United States military drops atomic bombs on the Japanese cities of Hiroshima and Nagasaki. These bombings—which Truman will call "the hardest decision I ever had to make"—remain to this day the only use of nuclear weapons in combat. On August 15, Japan surrenders to the United States and Allied nations.

1947: Al Capone dies on January 25.

LEARNING MORE ABOUT FRANKLIN ROOSEVELT AND AL CAPONE

"Al Capone at Alcatraz."
https://www.alcatrazhistory.com/cap1.htm.

Choldenko, Gennifer. *Al Capone Does My Shirts*. New York: Puffin Books, 2014.

"FDR Biography." Franklin D. Roosevelt Presidential Library and Museum.
https://fdrlibrary.org/fdr-biography.

Freedman, Russell. *Children of the Great Depression*. Clarion: 2005.

Huddle, Lorena. *Franklin D. Roosevelt*. New York: Britannica Educational Publishing, 2017.

Krull, Kathleen. *A Boy Named FDR: How Franklin D. Roosevelt Grew Up to Change America*. illus. by Steve Johnson and Lou Fancher. Knopf, 2011.

Mann, Lina. The "Sunshine Special": The Presidential Cars of Franklin D. Roosevelt. The White House Historical Association (October 14, 2017):
https://www.whitehousehistory.org/franklin-roosevelts-presidential-cars-1.

PBS. "Prohibition."
http://www.pbs.org/kenburns/prohibition/.

Smithsonian Channel. "Why Al Capone Wasn't Your Typical Discreet Gangster." (3-minute video).
https://www.smithsonianmag.com/videos/category/history/why-al-capone-wasnt-your-typical-discreet-g/.

Smithsonian. National Museum of American History. "The New Deal." American Enterprise Exhibition.
http://americanhistory.si.edu/american-enterprise-exhibition/corporate-era/new-deal.

U.S. Federal Bureau of Investigation. "Al Capone." History: Famous Cases & Criminals.
https://www.fbi.gov/history/famous-cases/al-capone.

Yancey, Diane. *Al Capone*. New York: Lucent, 2003.

MICHAEL GARLAND is the illustrator of more than 75 children's picture books, half of which he has also written. *Miss Smith and the Haunted Library* is a *New York Times* bestseller. Other recent books include *Daddy Played the Blues* (Notable Social Studies Trade Book for Young People), *Car Goes Far, Fish Had a Wish* (PW starred review), *Grandpa's Tractor* (selected for the Original Art of Children's Book Show by the Society of Illustrators in NYC), *Birds Make Nests* (Correll Children's Picture Book Award; Outstanding Science Trade Book, NSTA and CBC; Bank Street Best Children's Book), and *A Season of Flowers* (TD Summer Reading Club Top Recommended Read). Michael makes school visits across the country and can be found at www.garlandpicturebooks.com.

Thanks to Judith E. Stokes, reference librarian, and Gale Eaton, retired director of the University of Rhode Island Graduate School of Library and Information Studies, for their fact-checking and content reviews.

The front-cover image of Al Capone is based on an undated, uncredited photo from NYPL/Science Source.

Tilbury House Publishers
12 Starr Street
Thomaston, Maine 04861
800-582-1899 • www.tilburyhouse.com

Text and illustrations © 2019 by Michael Garland

Hardcover ISBN 978-088448-620-6
eBook ISBN 978-9-88448-622-0

First hardcover printing January 2019

15 16 17 18 19 20 XXX 10 9 8 7 6 5 4 3 2 1

Library of Congress Control Number: 2018961078

Cover and text designed by Frame25 Productions
Printed in China through Four Colour Print Group, Louisville, KY